You are Simply Divine

A Handbook of Simple
Spiritual Practices
for Divine Connectivity

Reverend Marya L OMalley

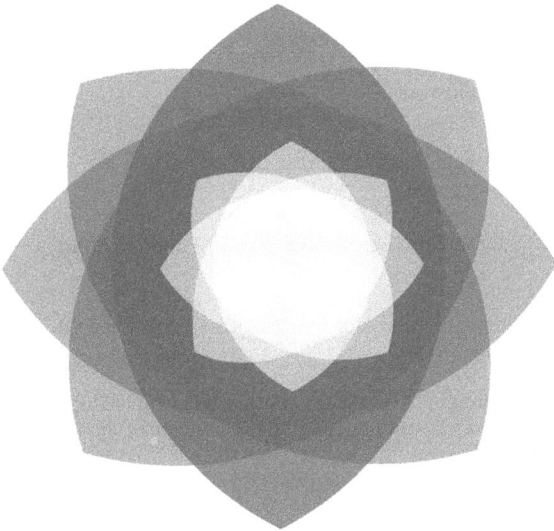

Cosmic Snap Publishing, LLC
Albuquerque, New Mexico

The author does not in any way directly or indirectly provide or dispense medical or psychological advice through this book, listed links, or resource lists. The author does not prescribe the use of any practice or information in this book as a form of treatment for physical, emotional, or medical problems. This information should not be used as or considered to be a substitute for medical or psychological care by a licensed health care professional. How you use the information in this book including the links and resources is at your own discretion, the author and publisher assume no responsibility for your actions. The intent of this author is to offer general information in your quest for spiritual well-being.

Cosmic Snap Publishing, LLC
5901 San Mateo Boulevard NE #211
Albuquerque, NM 87109
www.CosmicSnap.com

Book Layout ©2016 Cosmic Snap Publishing, LLC
Stylistic Editor Janice Lee Bush

Library of Congress Cataloging-in-Publication Data

OMalley, Marya
You are Simply Divine: A Handbook of Simple Spiritual Practices for Divine Connectivity / Marya L. OMalley.

First edition. | Albuquerque, New Mexico : Cosmic Snap Publishing [2016] , | Spirituality: Non-fiction | Includes bibliographical references and index.

Library of Congress Control Number: 2016903136
ISBN 978-0-9971520-0-5 (pbk. book)

Spiritual handbook — meditating — praying — blessing — journaling

Before I begin

Dear Simply Divine Friends,

I can only call my inspiration for this book as *Divine*. Although I have cherished my spiritual guidance and practiced meditation for 20+ years, I had become inconsistent. Then a little over two years ago, I began to get messages and signs over and over from one source or another to *meditate*. Whether it came from a radio program, a conversation, a book that dropped in my lap, or even a license plate -- the message was clear -- meditate. A busy schedule, a crisis or two, fatigue, work, other interests -- I had plenty excuses to continue on without meditating during my day.

However the promptings became so persistent that I could no longer hold up with excuses. So on a balmy August afternoon, I sat down and meditated.

As I drifted into a deep state, messages started coming rapidly. I experienced a profound and loving connection with Divine Source. From that meditation I had a new mission -- to help others connect with The Divine. From my Divine Source came this handbook of simple spiritual practices that can fit into everyday life.

Use these practices to help uncover that brilliant Divine light within you. These practices can also strengthen other spiritual teachings you already carry within or have yet to learn.

Customize the practices to fit your lifestyle. Be inspired. Take what resonates with the Divinity within you; set aside the rest. I hope you enjoy these practices and living your simply Divine life.

Wishing you much happiness and success,

Marya OMalley
September 22, 2016
Albuquerque, New Mexico

DEDICATING

I dedicate this spiritual handbook to my husband, Rudy Matalucci, my children, grandchildren, and teachers with whom I arrived at this special place to share my love and knowledge to help people consciously experience the inner Divine in daily life.

ACKNOWLEDGING

I thank the many family, friends, and mentors who inspire me on a daily basis and who encouraged me to write this book.

A special mention goes to those of you for helping me fine tune the text and practices with your watchful hearts. To name a few:

> Jami Morgan, Gabe Greenberg, Winona Fetherolf, Susan Gaustad, Jane Crabtree, Karen Sorel, Sonya Aguilar, Rudy Matalucci and Jan Bush for serving as my stylistic editor for this spiritual handbook.

I also wish to acknowledge many of my mentors/teachers and friends who have helped me on my path to my Divine self.

Thank you:

> Mom, Dad, Anna Theresa Clasemann, Frank Delsing, Gail Mayerchak, Dr. Adam Crabtree, Jim Downes, Janet Marinelli, Father Tom Weston, Sandy White, Shari Adkisson, Karen Ellen Smith, Janet Richmond, Meisha Monteil, Dr. David Rusoff, Louise Rusoff, Mary Robinson, Myrtle and Charles Fillmore, Mew, JuJu Bean, and the stranger at the YMCA.

And thank you, Divine Source of All.

How to use your new
Spiritual Handbook

Congratulations on owning your new spiritual handbook. Treat it with the intention to learn and grow from the words on these pages. I've laid it out to provide ample space for you to write in the margins, highlight special passages, and record your thoughts while connecting to your Divine Life.

These Simply Divine practices I've highlighted in this handbook can be performed by anyone. No equipment needed. You can do them in the comfort of your home while some can be practiced at your office desk.

I've divided the handbook into three parts – Discovery, Practicing, and Living. The chapters within these parts will help guide you through learning about The Divine you, connecting to The Divine within you, and incorporating The Divine you into your everyday life. References, including words and their meanings, follow.

Feel free to approach this book as best fits you. You can practice as you go, read the entire book and then reflect back, or skip around. Your choice.

Spiritual practices are meant to help you increase your awareness and connectedness to The Divine. Most people find that focusing on one or two methods works best.

My hope for you is over time, you will come to know and enjoy spiritual practice as a part of your everyday life.

Enjoy your Divine,

Marya OMalley

TABLE OF CONTENTS

That which ever was, is, and shall be
The One Originating Source Energy: The Divine.

--Marya L. OMalley
Minister, teacher, writer, chiropractor, life coach

PART 1: DISCOVERY

You are not IN the universe;
you ARE the universe, an intrinsic part of it.
Ultimately you are not a person, but
a focal point where the universe
is becoming conscious of itself.
What an amazing miracle.

-- Eckhart Tolle
Spiritual Teacher and Author

CHAPTER ONE: WHO ARE YOU?

You are The Divine.

You are Originating Source Energy – that which always was and ever shall be.

Your life – your entire being – serves as a focal point of this Energy. Your Divine Energy is active and conscious inside you.

Divine Energy expresses itself through your personal and impersonal selves.

Your **personal self** serves as the face that you present to the world. It stems from your ego, a part of your personality. Your experiences in the past, present, and future can affect your personal self – how much depends on you.

The **impersonal Self** serves as the authentic eternal Divine you. Self now is, always was, and always will be you. The essence of soul evolution expands your awareness of Divine Impersonal Self. You determine how much influence your impersonal Self has on your life. The more, the better.

It truly is that simple – you are simply Divine.

With this handbook, I intend to help you enhance your consciousness of The Divine Self within you. The spiritual practices that follow in Part 2 offer ways to consciously connect with The Divine you.

Everything that you have experienced and hoped for has led you to this moment; this is your path and You are on it.

--Marya L. OMalley
Minister, teacher, writer, chiropractor, life coach

Chapter Two: Why are you here?

You are here as soul embodied to be more conscious – to expand your awareness through discovery and evolve your Divine reality.

Your purpose is to become more and more aware of Divine expression within you, through you, all around you, and *as you*.

Consciousness is awareness

Evidence of **consciousness** is the observer in you – the part of you that knows what you are thinking, doing, and dreaming. Your present consciousness is your **awareness**. Being present unites your awareness of the infinite spiritual world with your awareness of your finite, physical world. Through consciousness we connect with The Divine.

Sometimes we will sense incompleteness because of the body's physical limitations. Often this lack, or limitation, will connect you to something else. How would you know darkness without light? How would you know light without darkness? These contrasting experiences are abundant in the physical world. I'm sure you thought of many more like hot/cold, hard/soft, etc.

In the physical realm objects are relatively fixed. When I set down my teacup, I expect it to stay there unless someone or something moves it. We can manipulate objects, change our environments, and experiment with things over time. Because of this relatively fixed nature, we can make clear choices to consciously develop our physical world.

A few years ago my business office, consulting area, and treatment room for my patients were together in one room. When I review patient files I normally spread them out on my desk to compare progress and identify needs. When it was time to see a patient in the office, I would hastily gather the papers and place them in my desk drawer. After jumbling my patient's papers like that, I had to start the patient file review anew by spreading them out again.

We found space for me -- a room too small to be a treatment room yet large enough to be an office.

My new office sat behind a door that had been locked long before I arrived. I'd never given it much thought. When I opened the door, I stepped into an office frozen in time.

For at least nine years the door had been locked and the office untouched. Everything was just as it was when the door was last closed. Papers were on the desk. Notes were tacked on the bulletin board. Old administrative files were bulging in the file cabinets. The plug-in calculator still worked. A film of dust covered everything and as you can imagine, the air was stale.

Nothing had changed as nobody had changed it.

Contrast this with the non-physical, mental realm where a thought instantaneously transports us to whatever we are thinking. For example, when you want to meditate in a lush green meadow from the confines of your living room; you mentally picture yourself in such a place. You concentrate on sensing through sight, sound, smell, touch, and taste.

You likely know or have heard about people who have near death experiences. These individuals recall visiting with relatives who live thousands of miles away, viewing another part of the hospital from above, looking down on themselves, and more all in the short time of "clinical death." Everything rests in The Divine You.

We are beautiful souls of Spirit that come here and hang out in a physical body for a period of time. Our bodies serve as instruments and temples of The Divine God.

I am not advocating that you dash about declaring, "I am God." If that were the case, you'd be doing something else like creating a new galaxy instead of reading this handbook. Remember...

As a wave is a part of the ocean,
so you are a part of The Divine ocean.

Your relationships

Relationships with people greatly enhance your life in both the finite physical world and the infinite spiritual world. Your bond with animals, places, and even things can play an important part to your evolving soul.

Relationships make possible the tremendous amount of learning that takes place in a lifetime. Among all the relationships that you have in your lifetime, the challenging ones usually will account for most of the learning and growing of your Divine Soul. At the same time, the easy and healthy relationships will provide you with the most happiness and satisfaction.

Your choice

Your soul rejoices at the opportunity to express through your body. Your soul serves your physical body as your conscious and subconscious minds -- the entire spectrum of your awareness. You can choose to be aware of your body and soul -- or not.

Think of this awareness like when you watch a movie. You become involved in the story – you suspend any doubt and go along with the plot whether real or make believe. You might be inspired, frightened, sad, or find yourself laughing out loud. You allow yourself to be immersed in the story so that you can experience the message being offered on that flat screen.

Stay aware of messages from your Soul to be inspired.

Your path

Everything that you have experienced and hoped for has led you to this moment; this is your path and you are on it.

As you find your way around the uncharted territory in your Divine mystery, allow your intention to be your compass. **Intend to create the world you want to live in.**

Accept contrasts. Contrast can help you decide which path to take. Every act of "free will" ultimately is about contrasting choices and decisions which hopefully lead you to a deeper Divine connection with your true Self.

Your soul community

In addition to guidance from your relationships in the physical world, help comes to you from the spiritual world. Divine Source guides you directly through spiritual messengers such as your own guardian angel, higher beings, and other higher aspects of yourself.

These helpers make up your "soul community" and constantly surround you in spirit. We each have our own community. In addition to angels, guiding spirits can include our ancestors, close friends, and spiritual masters we meet through their writings, videos, and podcasts. Your soul community stays with you in this simply Divine adventure!

For much of my life I did not understand soul community. I was afraid to ask for spiritual guidance because I didn't know where the advice might be coming from. I am no longer afraid because I invite only these loving beings working in concert with The Divine to guide me.

At your invitation your soul community will assist you in adapting to higher frequencies, connecting to The Divine within, and expanding your spiritual consciousness.

Divine Source will use your soul community, and a myriad of other avenues, to answer your prayers. Know that sometimes the one who hears the call and can answer our prayer is one of our own human contemporaries. Divine guidance comes in all forms.

Asking for help from your soul community is like asking for help from loving friends and family in the physical world. Only the highest good is served by your loving soul community.

Think of this guidance as spiritual gifts.

Instinct, free will, and Divine Will

What about our friends in the animal kingdom? Do animals have free will? In this humans are unique. Animals act primarily out of **instinct**. Instinctively dogs sniff other dogs, birds build nests, and horses head back to the barn after the trail ride.

The only truly free will kingdom is the human kingdom. **Free will** gives you the ability to make choices on your own. They are not determined by Divine intervention or by instincts. Free will plays a major role in our Soul's evolution. Through our free will choices, we determine the life we live.

We reach higher aspects of ourselves through **Divine Will**. Our soul community helps us rise above ego by Divine Will inserting the pure spirit of love and energy into our being. Our guardian angels help us carry out Divine Will.

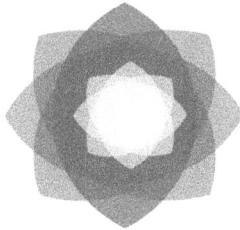

*The belief that whatever you've been is
what you have to be is a meme – a mind virus.*

-- Wayne Dyer
Author and Motivational Speaker

Chapter Three: Your evolving Soul

I like to compare our evolving souls to the biological metamorphosis of a butterfly. The butterfly starts out as an egg and becomes a caterpillar. The caterpillar encases itself in a cocoon and later emerges as a shimmering butterfly.

Just as the caterpillar is destined to be a butterfly; you are destined to emerge with a new expanded consciousness.

Sabotaging your spiritual growth

Many people, like me, get discouraged when they try to suppress negative emotions inside themselves or submerge into negativity longer than necessary.

Denial blocks us from true self-expression and experience. When we "feed" and prolong negative emotions, we block any pathway to happiness.

Most of us have experienced a loss of a love relationship. You probably thought your world had crumbled.

At the time, you likely felt various emotions – grief, anger, and loneliness to name a few. These feelings are natural. You can try to deny them and bully your way to happiness. You can also dwell in the sadness of love lost and swear you will never again trust anyone and will never be vulnerable again.

Between denial of and dwelling on these negative emotions exists a middle ground.

Middle ground of acceptance

Middle ground is a place where you can identify and observe your emotions. From this place of awareness, you can choose to accept what is and forgive yourself rather than criticize yourself.

This is also the place from which you can gain a better understanding of your Divine self.

When you feel negative emotions...

- ♥ Think about the situation that caused these feelings.

- ♥ Identify how you can benefit from the situation that caused these negative emotions.

- ♥ Ask yourself what you learned about yourself that can make you a better, stronger, more spiritual person.

- ♥ Imagine how you can consciously move forward with your life, free of denial and out of the "soup" of emotional turmoil.

Enjoy your metamorphosis!

At some point you'll look back at a situation and think, "Why did I fret and worry so much? Everything turned out well."

You'll eventually realize that there is no cause for worry, for you are simply Divine. You are here for a purpose, and you are fulfilling that purpose right now.

If you are wondering where to go and what to do, ask Divine Love and Wisdom to show you the way.

You have to invite Divine Love and Wisdom and your assistants in the higher realms to guide you in order to receive your answer.

Think about what you would most like to know in this moment -- and ask the question. The answer may be instantaneous or you may receive it in time. Whenever the answer comes – relax until then.

Know you are fully accepted and loved -- physically, spiritually, emotionally, and mentally.

Another beauty of your soul evolution is that it benefits everyone because we are all One. Yet we are all spiritually unique, just as our DNA is unique to our bodies. As the ocean is a vast accumulation of drops of water; how could anyone say which drop is most important?

Calling on The Divine Source

Naming and calling upon The Divine helps you to consciously call up The Divine Presence within yourself.

Your call clears your mind, making way for The Divine Presence to make itself known to you.

Divine Presence, the Universe, Ultimate Force, Holy Spirit, Originating Source, Great Spirit, Divine Source, God, Goddess, and Great Spirit are just some of the names for *the One*.

I use several names interchangeably, varying my call according to the nature of my invitation. Use whatever name or names resonate with you and your situation.

Chanting The Divine name

Chanting is an age-old spiritual practice in various religions and cultures the world over. Many believe the sound of The Divine name is sacred.

Through chanting we can actually feel The Divine Self.

Creation stories often account for the manifestation of worldly things and events by calling on "the Word" to create them. It is not a specific word; it is the sound -- the vibration that holds the sacred creative power within you.

In the past some religions forbade the saying of God's name aloud. Spiritual historians believe the prohibition had a mundane, political purpose: to prevent the common people from having the power held by the clergy.

Jonathan Goldman in his book, *The Divine Name*, tells us that there is actually no directive against saying The Divine name in scriptures such as the Torah. Rather, these writings state that we are to remember The Divine name and respect it.

*Your brain and your body are no longer a record of the
past. They are a map to the future –
a future that you've created in your mind.*

-- Dr. Joe Dispenza
Researcher, Chiropractor, Lecturer and Author

Chapter Four: Your spiritual growth

As infinite eternal souls, we're wired for further spiritual growth. Our physical bodies provide an exquisite Divine instrument to experience life in all its spiritual and physical glory. Planet earth is an amazing place!

Remember

Because we are infinite Spirits residing as souls in finite bodies, we must remember and connect with our Divine Will.

When we have a feeling of longing as if we're missing out, know that it's time to directly connect with our spiritual family soul community and our Creator.

In order to do this, we must ask for guidance and intend to follow it. Why? Because remember, the human kingdom is a "free will" kingdom. God and loving higher order beings like our guardian angels will only help us when asked; when they are wanted.

Love yourself

It all comes down to Love -- engaging in spiritual practice is Love. You are loving yourself and loving The Divine One when you connect with your Divine Self.

Spiritual practice:
- ♥ Connects you with your higher Self and soul community
- ♥ Reconnects you with your true Divine nature
- ♥ Replaces bad habits and excuses with loving intentions
- ♥ Quiets the mind and neutralizes negative thinking
- ♥ Frees you from constant ego domination

Spiritual practice does:

- o   not Remove challenges from your life
- o   not Make you immune from illness or injury
- o   not Cure all diseases and/or conditions
- o   not Protect you from loss
- o   not Keep your body from changing as you grow older
- o   not Eliminate your ego or your personal self
- o   not Make you superior to anyone else

Trying too hard can sabotage your practice. Relax and let it flow naturally. Simply...

- ♥   Make a commitment to practice daily
- ♥   Set aside time to practice; schedule it if you have to
- ♥   Let go of preconceived notions and emotional investments
- ♥   Pull in your attention when it wanders
- ♥   Breathe in and out – just breathe

Elements of spiritual practice

In my experience, spiritual practice is best when it includes these four components.

Physical –Physical anchoring helps us slip into the meditative state. When you meditate in the same physical position each session, this can facilitate your proper state of mind. Remember to accommodate to your schedule or location.

It is important that the chosen physical position feels good for you. If sitting cross-legged hurts your knees, don't do it. If sitting upright for more than a few minutes aggravates chronic back pain, lie down. Choose an environment that is best for you, your surroundings, and your spiritual practice.

Mental – A mental attitude of willingness helps you notice random thoughts, body sensations, and feelings free from judgment. Your mental state allows your inward thoughts to come and go like clouds crossing the sky.

You might have some amazing experiences, soaring moments of insight, or breath-taking visions. On the other hand, you might not notice much of anything. Whatever comes, avoid clinging to it; let it go.

Honesty – Practice honesty. Your inner guidance system knows if you are lying to yourself -- and so does The Divine within you.

Commitment – Some degree of commitment is required. Consider carefully your ability and willingness to commit your time. Remember, this is a commitment for you.

Initial enthusiasm may entice us to overcommit. Instead, commit to being more mindful of one normal practice in your day. Then eventually set aside at least four minutes of spiritual practice at a consistent time every day. You may choose to up your time commitment – five minutes, ten minutes, 30 minutes, or even more. Benefits come no matter how much time you choose to devote to daily spiritual practice.

Some people chose to spend an hour or more on daily spiritual practice. It's up to you how much time you have to devote. Remember to keep it simple and make it work for you. The last thing you want is to feel badly about your spiritual practice time.

You can also commit to practices scattered throughout the day. For example, as you make your morning tea or coffee -- choose to be mindful of your movements as you prepare the beverage, then mindful of the taste, the temperature, and the aroma as you savor it. Driving, bathing, and making your bed are some of the many actions that can incorporate your daily spiritual practices.

The Divine is already within you. The more you engage in spiritual practice, the more you expand your awareness of The Divine.

Intellectualizing

Like binge eating, mentally binging on something can harm you.

I remember when my daughter announced to me I was to be a grandmother. I had always thought this would be a glorious occasion for me – it was not. I felt upset with my daughter for breaking "cultural norms." She was young and unmarried. My plans and dreams for her squelched. My son followed the same path. Again, I was devastated.

I saw each grandchild's conception as being ill-timed, inconvenient, and irresponsible on the part of his or her parents. Intellectually I knew my children's "irresponsibility" at the time would make life harder for them and these precious babies.

That's all I could think about. I mentally binged on my emotional turmoil. I lived their irresponsibility and intellectualized on their missed opportunities.

Fortunately, I woke up. I finally saw how narrow my focus had been on pre-conceived assumptions and social norms that I had labeled "fact". My awakening allowed me to experience pure Love from my grandchildren. I could finally look at the situation through both my mind and heart.

Has it been harder on my daughter and my son by having their children at such young ages? Maybe. However, it has not been harder on me. Because of my free will to choose acceptance and Divine Will to choose love, my grandchildren now feed my soul and pluck my heartstrings.

Using your intellect

Do use your intellect – it's critical to think things through. As my story above shows, remember to work things through using both your head and heart together.

In the age of the internet and social media, misinformation can easily appear as "truth." Verify for yourself when possible.

This passage reminds me of something I learned as a child and carried with me for years: "Never assume anything; it makes an ass out of you and me."

Trust and verify; this applies in all areas of life from product claims to relationships to your own thinking.

The tyranny of unrealistic expectations

Some people talk about a constant state of blissful being -- as if they have concrete knowledge of it. Expecting to experience this constant state of being may derail your own success for Divine living.

Insights come and go. Ecstatic states of consciousness come and go -- if we have them at all. The human experience is one of ups and downs; light and darkness. Stop beating yourself up for being in difficult situations.

Soul evolution involves challenges. Challenges pave the path of your unfolding awareness. Jesus struggled with free will in the Garden of Gethsemane, the Dalai Lama faces many difficulties like being banned from his homeland, and Mother Theresa has had her doubts about her faith.

Expect to be challenged.

Head, hands, and heart

Balance your head, your hands, and your heart when approaching life's challenges.

Too often our minds bully our hearts which makes our hands compensate for the imbalance. When this happens, our "wheel of life" becomes lopsided and makes for an incredibly bumpy ride through life.

Intellectual self-bullying can lead us to confusion, frustration, and lack. It can cause us to go around and around analyzing everything and experiencing nothing.

Your mind, body, and spirit are meant to work in harmony.

Five major types of spiritual practice

Engaging harmoniously with your mind, body, and spirit in a quiet manner provides an essential dimension to your Divine Life. There are many ways to accomplish this experience. In this handbook, we'll discuss the five major types of spiritual practices.

1. Meditating
2. Praying
3. Blessing
4. Journaling
5. Moving

Choose the spiritual practice, or practices that resonate with you.

Let's begin.

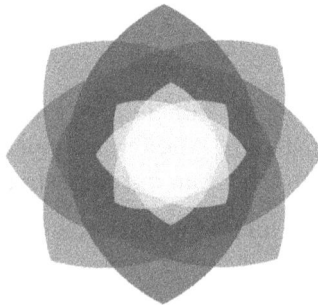

Your thoughts...

Remember:
As you engage in spiritual practice,
you are expanding your awareness of The Divine.

--Marya L. OMalley
Minister, teacher, writer, chiropractor, life coach

PART 2: PRACTICING

Life is only available in the present moment.

--Thich Nhat Hanh
Zen Master

CHAPTER FIVE: MEDITATING WAYS

What is meditation? Meditation focuses your attention inward.

When meditating you listen to The Divine while in prayer you talk with The Divine. There are many different ways to meditate, choose the best way for you to listen to The Divine within you.

The six most common ways of meditating include:

1. Watching the breath
2. Using sounds and mantras
3. Contemplating and reflecting
4. Focusing on the gap between your thoughts
5. Being mindful and aware
6. Taking a guided tour

I'll walk you through these various ways of meditating.

Test drive to choose one or two which works best for you. Most of us find that being consistent will make it easier to enter into a meditative state because we repeat established patterns. It's similar to walking to a coworker's office you visit often, and realizing you're there without remembering how you got there.

1. Watching the breath

An eager student once asked a master how to meditate. The master replied, "Breathe in, breathe out."

In this most basic form of meditation, you'll focus your attention on breathing. The preferred method is to breathe through your nose; breathing through your nose or mouth will work.

Practice: Watching the Breath

♥ Find a comfortable position that you can relax in for the length of time you plan to meditate. Many people prefer to sit with their legs crossed; others prefer to lie down.

♥ Take a few deep breaths in and out – slowly inhaling and exhaling. Relax as you do so.

♥ Now with each breath, focus your mind either on the sensation of the breath coming in and going out, or on the rising and falling of your belly as you breathe.

♥ Remain relaxed and continue to focus your awareness on your breath -- in and out.

These simple instructions may remind you of "wax on, wax off" when the *Karate Kid* realized how difficult, and later how important, it can be at times to stay focused on an uncomplicated act like breathing.

I recommend that you do this meditation for one minute; then add time as you wish. Make it a part of your daily routine.

You can also use **watching your breath** when you are feeling scattered, upset, or indecisive at any time during your day. Take a break to shift your focus from swirling thoughts to the slower rhythmic tide of your breathing in the present moment. It works.

2. Using sounds and mantras

Since ancient times, people have been using sounds and mantras to help them concentrate while meditating – listening to your Divine. In the 1970s, this form of meditation became popularized in the West and continues today.

Sound meditation can be in the form of chanting, humming, or singing. In mantra meditation, a word or phrase such as "Om" or "I am" is repeated as a vehicle for meditating.

The sound or mantra can be silent or out loud.

If you do your meditations out loud, you will notice how your body vibrates. You may even have the experience of wondering where the sound is coming from -- yourself or all around you. This can be a unifying experience of Oneness.

You choose your own mantra. For this practice, you can use one of my favorites.

Practice: Using sounds and mantras

- ♥ Find a comfortable position that you can relax in for the length of time you plan to meditate.
- ♥ Take a few deep breaths in and out – slowly inhaling and exhaling. Clear your mind as you do so.
- ♥ Repeat your mantra:
- ♥ I am one with Divine Love and Wisdom
- ♥ Continue to repeat your mantra until you lose your thoughts and time has passed.

In a group, sound meditation can be very powerful. Recorded chants and sound meditations are available from many sources. In the back of the book you will find more resources for this type of meditation.

3. Contemplating and reflecting

In this type of meditation, you choose a word, phrase, or passage to focus your reflection on The Divine. Many religious ceremonies use this type of meditation.

Again, you can read out loud or in silence.

As you read, place your attention on the essence of the words; what was the author intending to convey? How do these words speak to you and you alone? Remember, you are listening. Choose your passage wisely.

You can choose one word or inspirational quotes, thoughts, phrases, poems, and passage from a book. You can choose to contemplate on a short passage reading it multiple times, or a whole chapter. The choice is yours to make.

For example, Rabbi Aryeh Kaplan writes about contemplative meditation on the stars. This is based on the Biblical verse, "Lift your eyes on high and see who created these [stars]? The One who brings out their host and numbers them, calling them all by name..." Isaiah 40:26. You can read more in his book *Jewish Meditation: A Practical Guide*.

Practice: Contemplating and reflecting

- ♥ Select your reading. Get in a comfortable position, read or speak the selection to yourself while reflecting on the meaning. Breathe in...breathe out. Repeat.

- ♥ If you chose a longer passage, read one line or even just one phrase. Take a break to breathe in...breathe out. Read the next sentence or phrase. Breathe in...breathe out. Repeat this until the entire passage has been covered or to start over again.

If your attention wanders, gently return to your selected focus and notice what comes. Repeat as often as you want.

4. Focusing on the gap between your thoughts

Author, life coach, radio program host, and speaker -- Alan Cohen encourages us to "hang out" in the gap between thoughts to find God – our Divine.

Present moment experience exists in the space between our thoughts -- the silence within. This experience has been referred to by many spiritual teachers as "The Silence" or "The Stillness."

You may have heard this quote from Psalms 46:10: "Be still, and know that I am God!" Japa meditation uses repetition of a prayer or mantra to bring one to that space. This gap of stillness can open your conscious experience of The Divine.

Practice: Entering The Gap / The Silence

- ♥ Place your left hand over your heart center and your right hand over your left. Your heart center rests in the center of your chest between your breasts at the mid sternum or breastbone.

- ♥ As you breathe in say to yourself, "I am of God." Hold your breath for a few seconds, then exhale. Repeat this 5 times.

- ♥ Now center your attention softly on your heart center. Allow thoughts to come and go. Remain in calm attention. You could say to yourself something like, "I wonder when my next thought will come." Or "What might my next thought be?" A space will open.

- ♥ You will enter the gap, the place between thoughts. This is the gap, void of thought. It is in this silence where Divine Presence resides.

- ♥ Feel how pleasant it is -- to be with your Divine Source in solitude and happiness. Nothing else to do; nowhere else to be -- just you and the One. Repeat this as often as you like and do it for as long as you like.

5. Mindfulness Meditation

Mindfulness meditation heightens your awareness through focused attention. Through this meditation, you become aware of what is in the present.

Mindfulness can be applied to any restful state or activity -- even eating. You'll find mindfulness meditation especially useful for focusing on physical sensations and deliberate movements. Mindfulness and awareness will serve you in many forms of meditation. Two examples of mindfulness as a spiritual practice:

- ♥ Walking Meditation
- ♥ Self-awareness

Walking Meditation

In the walking meditation practice, you are going to walk. You can walk outside in nature or inside a busy place like a mall. What matters is that you feel comfortable and want to be there walking. You can do this alone or silently with a friend. Many people make this a spiritual practice as they walk their dogs in the mornings.

Practice: Walking Meditation

- ♥ Walk upright and focus on your walking. Notice how your legs rise, your knees bend, and your feet land on the ground. Notice any details, however small, that come into your awareness of walking.

- ♥ Feel the temperature surrounding you. Feel the weight of your legs, hands, and feet. Feel the ground, the pebbles under your feet. One by one, notice each breath you take.

- ♥ Whatever comes up, notice it and let it go.

- ♥ Be aware that the observer in you -- your conscious Impersonal Self -- is doing the noticing.

♥ Whether you know it or not, your impersonal Self is always aware. It is watching and observing all that you do because you are consciousness. You are The Divine consciousness itself.

♥ Begin this walking meditation for 10 minutes or so. You can keep at that level or increase the time as you wish.

Self-awareness Meditation

The self-awareness meditation is meant to help you get back in touch with your sensations and feelings. You can use self-awareness meditation to release what seems to be stuck in your body. It is difficult, if not impossible, to experience Divine connection if you are disconnected from mind, body, or spirit.

If some old feelings or memories surface that overwhelm you or appear too powerful for you to process yourself, you may want to consult with a therapist. Sometimes help is needed with those feelings and memories which have adverse effects in present time. Like therapy, this spiritual practice will not erase memory.

Your objective for self-awareness meditation is to release negative effects that have accumulated over time and to create a new perspective to guide you. Let's begin.

Practice: Self-Awareness Meditation

♥ Get comfortable in a place where you will be free from disturbance during the time of this spiritual exercise. You may sit or lie down. Your clothing should be loose and comfortable. Close your eyes or softly gaze at a point several feet in front of you.

♥ Start by breathing in. Notice the sounds around you, the sounds further away from you, and while exhaling, allow these sounds to drift in and out as they naturally do. Continue to breathe in and out calmly and slowly. Now notice any thoughts that you are having. Let them come and go; no need to focus on them, simply watch your thoughts come and go.

♥ Now notice the surface on which you rest. Notice, as you continue to breathe in and out calmly and slowly, the texture of that surface. Maybe you feel it through your clothing or with your fingertips or some other part of your body. Simply notice and continue breathing in a calm and rhythmic fashion.

♥ Now notice how that chair, bed, ground, or floor supports you. You can trust that you will remain there for the rest of this session because it will be there for you.

♥ Starting with your fingernails, notice how it feels underneath your nails. Observe anything that becomes apparent to you. Let your attention spread to the rest of your fingers, noticing their position and any sensations you might be feeling through them and inside of them.

♥ Observe any thoughts and let them drift in and out. Relax more and more as you move through this spiritual exercise.

♥ Now shift your focus to your entire hand. Feel the inside of your hand and move up your arm. Feel the outside and any sensations, textures, or temperatures around it.

♥ Notice any thoughts you might be having. Simply allow them to drift in and out again. Continue breathing.

♥ Do the same with your shoulders, the muscles and tissues that connect your shoulders to your neck. What position are your shoulders in? Are they close to your neck and tensed up or are they relaxed and soft?

♥ Turn your attention to your back. Notice any sensations there or thoughts that occur to you.

♥ Next, observe how your neck feels. Is it tight or constricted? Or relaxed and soft? What is your neck telling you?

♥ Without judgment, notice and breathe.

♥ Now attend to your head and any sensations you feel there. Observe any thoughts that come up while focusing on your head. Focus on your face -- does it feel warm or cool? Soft or tense? Do any thoughts come up as you focus on your face?

♥ Using this same type of attention and relaxation, move down through the front of your body starting with the clavicles or collarbones, your chest, your breasts and down to your abdomen. Notice the sensations that each area feels and likewise feel that area from the inside- out.

♥ Notice if an area seems to be telling you something. Let those thoughts drift in and out.

♥ Continuing to breathe, move down through the organs and tissues in your lower abdomen. Notice any sensations, textures, temperatures, and feel from the inside out now, simply noticing.

♥ Simply notice any thoughts that you might be having as you move around your physical body. Allow them to come and go without judgment.

♥ Now move into your genital area. Notice any sensations, textures, temperatures, and feel your genitals from the inside out now, simply noticing.

♥ Move on to the perineum, the place between your genitals and your anal area. Notice its composition, notice how it supports your pelvic floor, notice any sensations, textures, temperatures, and feel from the inside of your perineum now, simply noticing. Simply notice any thoughts that you might be having. Allow them to come and go without judgment.

♥ Continue to breathe. Move on to your anal area. Notice any sensations, textures, temperatures, and feel your anal area from the inside out now, from the cavity there, inside the rim of your anus, simply noticing. And now notice any thoughts that you might be having. Allow them to come and go without judgment.

♥ As you continue to breathe slowly and rhythmically. move on to your hips and legs. Notice any sensations, textures, temperatures. Feel your hips and then your legs from the inside out now, simply noticing. Simply notice any thoughts that you might be having. Allow them to come and go without judgment. Do the same with your ankles and feet.

♥ Pay particular attention to the soles of your feet. Notice any sensations, textures, temperatures. Feel your feet and the soles of your feet from the inside out now --simply noticing. Any thoughts that you might be having, allow them to come and go without judgment. Notice your toenails and the sensations, feelings, textures, and temperatures there and feel them right underneath the toenails and now outward to beneath your feet.

♥ Breathing in and out; bring your awareness to your breath. Notice the air as it first enters your nostrils and then as it leaves on exhalations out through your nostrils. Repeat this breath awareness several times.

♥ Now breathe a big breath in through your nose and exhale through your mouth with a powerful "Ha-Ha-Ha" repeating as many times as you need to fully exhale.

♥ Now breathe a big breath in through your nose and exhale through your mouth with a powerful "AHHHHHH" sound until you fully exhale your breath, getting any stale air out of your lungs. Repeat this several times and relax.

Some people experience powerful emotions in parts of their bodies. People report getting messages or seeing images of past events that triggered part of their body to carry some emotion – which can be love, happiness, and confidence or it can be on the flip side of pain, anger, and grief.

If negative emotions became stuck, often it's because we did not feel safe enough at the time to express those emotions. It could also have been due to a real or perceived danger. Or, perhaps we were taught, "We don't show our feelings in this family."

Whatever the reason, stuck is stuck.

If you find you have stuck feelings that stop you from being the person you want to be, you may find it helpful to breathe into the area of pain or whatever negative emotion seems to be lodged there. Then exhale to release. This will help free your body from the influence of stagnated emotion.

You can also breathe into good emotions that you found on this spiritual exercise. Instead of freeing them from your body, give your good emotions permission to influence your personal self.

6. Guided meditation

Guided meditation is facilitated by a person in the room with you or via a live Internet stream, podcast, or other type of recording.

In guided meditation as a spiritual practice, the meditation is facilitated -- not dictated. The value will be in your own inner experience.

Select a guide that you believe will enhance your Divine connectivity. Feel free to try different guides before you find the guide or guides who seem to be a good fit for you.

I found that after following the same guided meditation several times, that I have it "recorded" in my mind. Often I simply listen to the "recording" in my mind. Some people choose to continue with the recording for the inductive musical background or simply for the ease of it.

Another way to do guided meditation is to record a meditation yourself, such as the example below. Your own voice will be your guide when meditating.

When I am tired or unwell, I find guided meditation especially helpful because I can just lie back and listen. In addition to www.YouAreSimplyDivine.com, I have listed some guided meditation resources in the Appendix. You can also find guided meditations on your smart phone as apps. You can make these available as you move through your day.

The guided meditation that I give below is an example of what might be said by a guide or recorded by you for your own use.

I have pre-recorded this guide available for download for free on my website. Go to **www.YOUAreSimplyDivine.com.**

Practice: Simply Divine Guided Meditation

- Get in a comfortable position for meditation. Breathe in through your nose and out through your mouth. Breathe another time releasing your worries, hopes, and concerns as you exhale.

- Place your attention at the area of your heart center in the center of your chest at your heart level. Breathe into your heart center saying to yourself, "I embody Divine Love and Wisdom."

- As you exhale, relax into yourself and imagine a beautiful light in your heart. This light is The Divine eternal light. It always has been, and always will be, with you.

- As you focus on this light, allow it to expand, filling your entire heart center. Let your Divine eternal light extend through your body, down your legs to the tips of your toes and up your body, front and back, to the crown of your head.

- Continue to breathe rhythmically in and out as your Divine light expands beyond your physical body, outward all around you, beneath and above you.

- Simply remain in this light, bathing in its radiance, feeling the warmth, love and wisdom of this Divine light. Observe, allow, and relax without judgment -- simply be.

- Relax for several minutes...

- Gently return your attention to your breath for a few rhythmic inhalations and exhalations as The Divine light centers once again peacefully within your heart.

- Open your eyes.

*"Prayer in its simplest form
is any conscious attempt to
experience the presence of God."*

- Mary-Alice and Richard Jafolla
Spiritual Authors and Golf Enthusiasts

Chapter Six: Initiating Prayer

We define prayer as conversing with The Divine Spirit. As with any type of conversation, prayer also involves listening. The listening aspect is where prayer and meditation overlap.

Prayers can be prayers of thanksgiving or praise. Prayers can ask for help. Prayers can request that "Divine Will be done." Prayers can also be invitations that you offer to Divine Source.

What is your intention? What do you desire? You can ask Divine Presence to expand your awareness for greater clarity, to experience your own true radiant Divine nature, or to fulfill whatever your heartfelt longing might be.

Divine Source and its messengers, beings of the higher realms, will only help you if you invite them to you. An emergency might involve a very quick subconscious invitation! It is your free will to invite these higher beings to your aid for guidance, to comfort you, to inspire you, and to better experience your Divine Self.

If you wish to end an addiction, ask The Divine to help you. You will receive help. You must accept this help and welcome the change in you. Countless numbers of people have received help; many have told their stories of this healing process.

One of the most powerful ways to ask for help is through the Holy Spirit. Ask the Holy Spirit -- Divine wisdom, knowledge, and understanding -- to inspire your every thought, word and deed. In art, we often depict the Holy Spirit as a dove with radiant light surrounding us as it hovers overhead with incredible brilliance. Ask the Holy Spirit to hover over your head.

Prayer as spiritual practice

The types of prayer that I teach as spiritual practice include:

1. Affirmative prayer
2. Gratitude prayer
3. Centering prayer
4. Silence prayer

Entering into prayer

Many people find that it helps to initiate prayer in the same way each time to get into the most connected state.

I like to center my attention at my heart center and call upon The Divine Presence within. On exhalation, I release my worries and concerns. Then I say my prayers.

1. Affirmative prayer

In the New Testament Jesus says, "So I tell you, whatever you ask for in prayer, believe that you have received it, and it will be yours" (Mark 11:24).

The foundation of affirmative prayer is "...believe that you have received it."

Through your faith you affirm that what your desire already exists and is on its way. This form of prayer tends to change the thought pattern in the mind from a place of lack to a place of abundance.

This type of prayer became popular with the New Thought Movement that arose in the late 1800s and continues to flourish.

Practice: Affirmative Prayer

Entering the prayer state:

- ♥ Take a deep breath through your nose. As you exhale, release your worries, thoughts, and concerns. Inhale again, focusing on your heart center. Affirm, "I am simply Divine" or "I am of God." Exhale, releasing any tension. Repeat as needed.

- ♥ I find it helpful to place my hands over my heart center as I do this step. Feel free to choose another word or phrase that you feel best for entering your prayer state.

Affirming The Divine Presence:

- ♥ Continue breathing. Affirm, "The Divine flows through everything at all times." Or "The loving forces of Divine Wisdom support me now."

Recognizing The Divine Presence within you:

- ♥ Recognize that because The Divine flows through everything at all times, The Divine also flows through each person including you right now and always. "My body serves as a conduit for The Divine."

Realizing you are one with The Divine:

- ♥ In this step, realize that since The Divine flows through everything and everyone including you at all times, you acknowledge the truth, for example, "I am one with The Divine and I ask The Divine to bring the right words to my book to share with others." In this knowledge you realize The Divine lives in every aspect of your life so invite The Divine to help you.

Giving thanks:

- ♥ In this step feel grateful. You feel the beauty of The Divine connecting to your Divine nature – your spirit. If you don't feel it now, ask for Divine guidance again and again until you do. "I believe and give thanks for being one with The Divine."

Releasing yourself to go forth to do good:

- ♥ In this final step, you release your words into the hands of God/The Divine. "I let go and let God take me to the next step." Know that all that you have asked, with the intention of your highest good, will come to you. You have planted the seeds: "As you sow, so shall you reap."

2. Gratitude and praise prayers

You can easily engage prayers of gratitude and praise any time throughout your day. I do. This simple form of prayer heightens your awareness of Divine Source expressed in your life.

Have you ever wondered why a prayer before meals is called "grace"? Many people believe that the meal becomes holy by a prayer of giving thanks. Grace is a blessing from The Divine Source that we acknowledge through gratitude.

I also use the prayer before my meals as an opportunity to acknowledge The Divine in all that brought the food to the table: the sun, the rain, the fields, the seeds, the farmers, and all the people who harvest, transport, sell, and prepare the food that we eat. This simple prayer before meals serves as an example of Divine Order manifesting in our lives each day.

One of my favorite ways to pray with gratitude is to take a walk in nature. There is much to be thankful for -- even in the tiniest leaf on the ground.

Prayers of praise are often sung. Singing is a wonderful way to send and receive vibrations that resonate throughout our bodies. Prayers of praise have a way of cleansing our minds as they connect us with The Divine. Some people remember songs more easily than words alone.

Praise prayers can be simple prayers of any length that extend to the wonder of creation, to what is known and unknown, to the miracle and magic of The Divine, or whatever comes to you. Earlier in the book I mentioned the power of chanting The Divine name(s). This also is prayer.

Practice: Gratitude prayer in nature

♥   Go outside and place your attention on your breath. Think about the carbon dioxide that you exhale as breath to the plants that likewise "exhale" oxygen that is breath for you. Just as you are part of the natural cycle of life, you are also part of the natural cycle of The Divine.

3. Centering prayer

Centering prayer seeks to purposefully bring The Divine into our living lives, using verbal, mental or affective elements. It has been described as receptive "resting" in God.

The name for this type of prayer was coined in the 1970s. Centering prayer is based on Christian contemplative prayer that harks back to St. John of the Cross, Theresa of Avilla, and earlier mystics.

One of the modern founders of Centering prayer, Fr. Thomas Keating, explains that its essence is consenting to "God's presence and action within."

The prayer practice below consists of Fr. Thomas Keating's guidelines for simple centering prayer. See the appendix for the link to his article, *The Method of Centering Prayer.*

Practice: Centering Prayer

- ♥ Choose a **sacred word** as the symbol of your intention to consent to God's presence and action within you.

- ♥ Sit comfortably, close your eyes and settle in. Silently introduce your sacred word as the symbol of your consent to God's presence and action within.

- ♥ When you become aware of thoughts, return gently to your sacred word.

- ♥ At the end of the prayer period, remain in silence with eyes closed for a couple of minutes.

4. Silence prayer

When prayer is initiated as a conversation and then followed by immersion in silent listening, this is silence prayer.

Practice: Silence Prayer

- ♥ Engage in prayerful communication with The Divine. Then be still; sit in silence and listen. Rest in the stillness and let Divine Love surround you in the silence. In this sense, prayer becomes like meditation.

Praying for others

Praying for others can uplift you and enhance your awareness of your connection with The Divine. Praying for other people benefits you as well. Because we are all one, you are in essence, praying for yourself.

If you pray for another, pray affirmatively and release him/her into the hands of The Divine at the end of your prayer. It's important that you don't inadvertently tether him/her to the problem – or yourself! Release.

You must drop any attachment you might have to knowing someone's sad story -- feeling her/his pain or being awed by the "disaster" in her/his life. Refrain from speaking words of permission that allow him/her to remain stuck. "That's just terrible." "No one should have to bear this pain!"

Remember every experience can be used to help us in some way and ever so powerfully if we intend that to be so. Even those we think of as "bad" experiences. I have heard cancer survivors confess that the disease helped them to be a better person.

When you pray with and for someone, you must honor his or her integrity. If it is unclear what to pray for, ask for the highest good, the most beneficial outcome. The highest good, the most beneficial or better says it all without specifics. Trust that Divine Source will take care of the rest.

Praying with others will raise the power of your experience. If you are going to say repetitive prayers, know that they can be more powerful when your attention and positive intentions are present for The Divine Power to come through your prayers.

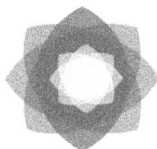

At its deepest level, blessing implies a sense of the sacred, of some hidden abundance available to those who open themselves up to it through this practice, of some unseen power available to protect and make whole.

- Pierre Pradervand
Author and Spiritual Leader

Chapter Seven: Blessing your life

As a spiritual practice, blessing powerfully enhances expression of The Divine. You can give blessing to everyone in any situation and as often as possible. Blessing means extending love to another.

David Spangler, author of *Blessing: The Art and Practice*, says that blessing is akin to remembering. To me this means remembering that we all have value, we are all connected, and remembering how good it feels to express Divine Blessing.

What matters when you bless is your intention to bless. A blessing can take many forms. It can be formal such as the blessing I give to a couple in a wedding ceremony. It can be the loving touch of my husband when he places his hand on mine.

Animals can give and receive blessings too. Mew, the cat, gave me his blessing by pressing his paws up and down softly on my chest. I blessed him as I stroked his fur.

When you bless, you are using your imagination to create the blessing. You are imaging well-being and love flowing to those being blessed.

Blessing can be done up close or faraway. It may or may not include physical touch. A gesture we have often seen in ceremony and portrayed in art includes the hands raised up, palms slightly cupped and angled forward toward those being blessed as though holding them in a sacred place.

Blessings can also be given from a distance in a letter, a phone call, a text, an email, or simply sent through the air.

Again, the necessary element is the intent to bless. With this intent, love is surely present. This creates a blessing presence.

A way to bless others when it is hard to do so, is to first extend a blessing that is universal. For example, the Buddhist expression, "May all sentient beings be happy."

Some Buddhists recommend starting with the blessing, "May I be happy," and then expanding the blessing outward more broadly to "May all be happy." Then you can be more specific and ask "May _____ be happy." It is a beautiful expression of self-honoring. When I am feeling reluctant to bless a specific person, I personally find the broad blessing works best.

The connection with your true Divine Self is disrupted when you withhold blessings and even blocked when outright wishing another ill. The Divine Self knows that we are all one and *to curse another is to curse oneself.*

Practice: Happiness Blessing

- ♥ May all beings be happy.
- ♥ May all my family and friends be happy.
- ♥ May all my co-workers be happy.
- ♥ May _____ (name of person) be happy.
- ♥ May I be happy.

Practice: Simple Blessings

- ♥ Bless this house.
- ♥ May your home be a loving haven for family and friends.
- ♥ God bless you.
- ♥ May you have a safe trip.

Practice: Irish Blessing

- ♥ May the road rise to meet you, the rain fall softly on your fields, the wind be at your back, and until we meet again, may you be held in the palm of God's hand.

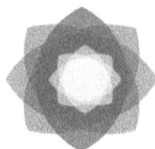

Bless you.

Journaling is a voyage to the interior.

--Christina Baldwin
Author, Speaker, and Educator

CHAPTER EIGHT: KEEPING YOUR JOURNAL

Keeping a journal as a spiritual practice helps you to remember, to receive insights into your thoughts and experiences, plus enhance your life. To journal as a spiritual practice involves reflection over reaction.

What do I mean by that? When reflecting you notice your feelings, moods, and thoughts. As a mirror reflects back an image, your reflection reveals an image of your inner consciousness.

Reaction on the other hand, is like a reflex. When I tap the tendon on your knee, a signal travels up the nerve to the spine and back down to your knee to cause your lower leg to jerk. That signal only travels to your lumbar spine. In this context, reaction is like a knee jerk reflex when your consciousness is not engaged.

You may find it useful to keep more than one journal. For example, keep one journal that expresses gratitude and another that reflects your thoughts on wise quotes.

Spiritual teachers often suggest journaling after meditation to record insights and observations you experienced.

This is what you do when you journal. You are recording God's grand, epoch-spanning redemptive story as it unfolds in your limited, temporal sphere of existence here on earth. Your journal has the potential to record the continuation of the Holy Spirit's work in our world!

--Adam L. Feldman
Pastor, Church Planter Coach, and Writer

As with any spiritual practice, find a quiet place to journal. Or, if you are like me, a place like a commuter train or a restaurant with indistinct hum of voices around to create some "white" noise will do quite nicely.

Saying a brief prayer and focusing on your breath can also help you enter a relaxed and conscious state for your journaling.

If you write by hand, choose a pen and paper that you enjoy. I am a great fan of gel pens. I love how the gel ink glides over paper.

Some people find journaling using a computer works best. They let their fingers on the keyboard transmit their thoughts.

Remember to allow enough time for your journaling to feel relaxed. Some set a timer to know when they have to move on to another activity. I prefer to allow things to flow and trust that I will have enough time for my writing.

Write in your own style. Let it be in your own voice. Journaling is your unique way of expressing your Divine. I never worry about punctuation or grammar when I journal. If I decide to blog about what I wrote, I edit it then.

As with everything today, "there's an app for that." In the Resources section I have listed some helpful apps for your smart phone gratitude journaling.

Practice: Journaling for Divine Living

- ♥ **Reflecting.** Chose an inspirational quotation, poem, or a passage from your favorite book. Reflect on the meaning. How does Divine Love and Wisdom speak to you through these words? How is the sacred in these words like the sacred within you? What observations, wisdoms, or questions arise in your thoughts? Write insights that come up. You may find that you spontaneously expand on the inspirational idea in your own way.

- ♥ **Thanking.** Think of someone or something for which you are grateful. Reflect on your gratitude and write about it. A life challenge can be a great jumping off place if you are feeling stuck. How are you grateful for a challenging person or situation? How has the Divine shown up as a result? Ask yourself if Divine Love and Wisdom were to show up in the challenging situation, how would that look? What would you learn? How would you benefit in some way?

- ♥ **Conversing.** Express your heartfelt thoughts and feelings to Divine Love. Try to focus on one thought or feeling. Listen to what comes up and journal the words of love, wisdom, and guidance that emerge.

- ♥ **Praying, meditating, walking, or sitting quietly.** After a reflecting activity, journal about your experience. What sensations did you have? Smells, sounds, sights, feelings? How do you feel now? Did you feel Divinely connected? What happened if you put your attention on past worries and complaints? How did you shift your attention back to the present moment of Divine Spirit?

The Journal as companion and as pathway

To many, their journal serves as a spiritual friend. A journal can also be a wonderful memento of your spiritual journey; a reminder of your Divine insights.

Like walking a labyrinth, your journal is an inward written path that brings your true Divine Self out into your conscious world.

[whether] we learn to dance by practicing dancing,
or to live by practicing living...
one becomes in some area an athlete of God.
--Martha Graham
Choreographer and Mother of Modern Dance

Chapter Nine: Moving your soul

Movement as a spiritual practice can take a variety of forms such as dance, yoga, spontaneous movement, housework, walking a labyrinth, and even sports. Any movement can be a spiritual practice. Movement becomes a spiritual practice when we consciously bring the soul into the movements of the body.

If you are an active person, this may be the ideal spiritual practice for you.

If you avoid exercise, integrating your soul through moving your body can also work for you.

As a regular spiritual practice, intention and attention are used to bring the soul into your movement. The late Gabrielle Roth in her book, *Sweat Your Prayers,* reminds us that physical movement is a potent spiritual act because our souls live inside our bodies.

Moving enlivens us!

When you move as a spiritual practice, it is especially important that you choose enjoyable movements that you can couple with focused awareness. Practices with slow, flowing movement include tai chi, yoga, and swimming. Running is an example of fast, flowing movement.

If exercise is already a part of your routine, make it a spiritual practice for you.

Practice: Exercise with Spirit

- ♥ Clear your mind chatter through focused attention on parts of the body and conscious movement as you exercise. Express a willingness to connect with The Divine through your body.

- ♥ Make an affirmative statement such as, "This body is a happy home for my soul," while you exercise.

- ♥ Place your attention on the exercise and consciously notice what is happening. Observe how mind, body, and spirit harmoniously present themselves.

- ♥ If harmony seems to be missing, simply listen and ask -- Is mind chatter distracting me? Am I clinging to an emotion that's blocking me? If so, practice clearing the mind and releasing distractions and negative emotions. Notice the change to a more harmonious blend of mind, body and spirit.

- ♥ Let your creative spirit fly and engage in spontaneous movement to music, prayer, or a mantra.

- ♥ Focus on your breath as you walk, run, or do other movements.

- ♥ Practice blessing as you exercise. For example, "Bless this Divine body." "I bless myself as a Divine creation."

- ♥ As you hike, become aware of your breath. Imagine that you are breathing in oxygen from the plants around you and giving them carbon dioxide to breathe. Notice that you are part of nature's creation.

- ♥ With any form of exercise affirm, "I am of Divine Creator, in one creation. I am at one with the Divine.

How about you athletes?

Athletic games and sports are great for spiritual practice. As you train, try some of the exercises mentioned above or make up your own as you work through your movements.

Research in sports psychology confirms the importance of visualizing before the game through meditation. You can enhance these practices by adding Divine Spirit.

Practice: Team Sports Pre-Game Warm Up

First, take a few moments to still mind chatter. Focus on your breath, breathing in through your nose to the count of 10, holding to the count of 4, and breathing out through your mouth to the count of 10. Repeat a few times until you feel relaxed and receptive. Notice your body and any tensions, aches or pains. Acknowledge them and let them go as you exhale.

Now imagine the golden eternal light of The Divine within your heart glowing and extending outward to your teammates and coaching staff. Imagine being connected and in sync with your team mates in this light field.

As you stretch and do pre-game warm up exercises, imagine that this light gets brighter, flowing like a powerful current through your body as you become more energized and aware. Imagine you and your teammates in sync with one another, moving with the ball, through the space around it, and connecting with the ball all in perfect timing. Imagine engaging fully in the challenge and fun of the game.

Prayer and movement

Be creative in prayer! Let your spirit fly!

- ♥ Combine a spontaneous prayer with movement.
- ♥ Combine traditional prayers with movement.
- ♥ Sing your prayers as you move.
- ♥ Move your hands as you pray.

Practice: Praying with Movement

- ♥ Stand and open your arms outward palms up-ward toward the sky, raise your arms until your palms touch and come together above your head.

- ♥ Keep them together and bring your palms in front of your heart center, now cross your hands, palms down over your heart center and say, "I am one with the Divine."

- ♥ Rejoin your palms, touching the tips to your lips as you pray, "Divine Presence, I am open to guidance in all that I say, do, and think."

- ♥ Notice what comes to you. When ready, cup your hands facing outwards and give thanks to Divine Love and Wisdom.

- ♥ Raise your palms up releasing your prayers throughout time and in all dimensions.

- ♥ Bring your palms back in front of your heart center and gently touching your lips say, "And so it is. Amen."

Adding Divine Spirit to Dance

Be assured anyone can dance. There is no right or wrong way to dance as spiritual practice. You can be a conditioned athlete, couch potato, or strapped in a wheel chair -- you can dance. Dance with your whole body or dance with your hands, toes, or eyes.

Practice: Spiritual Dance

1. Allow yourself space. You want to be able to dance about and freely move your legs and arms.

2. Play some music, sing, and pray while you dance.

3. Start by warming up. Do some wiggling movements, or move your body intentionally: bending, flexing, and rotating. Notice any tension or stiffness; release as much as possible – then dance.

4. Use your imagination to guide the dance.

    ♥ Imagine you are a deer leaping in the morning sun, the dew spraying from your hooves, as you feel full of life.

    ♥ Imagine you are a sunflower opening to the light, just as it is natural to open to the light of your true Divine nature.

    ♥ Imagine that you are dancing with The Divine.

5. Let your body guide you.

Experience the gap

Those who spiritually engage in movement often tell us of experiencing suspended time accompanied by the feeling of being "lost" in movement. They talk about becoming one with the music, being the ball, or their body soaring with their souls.

This is the Gap where you experience The Divine without filters. Embrace it.

Physical and spiritual connection

The revelation that physical movement and spiritual connection can be one may be profound to us Westerners. As children, most of us experienced a clear distinction between the two. Soccer was separate from Sunday school; dance classes had no relation to prayer. In fact, some friends were not allowed to dance at all.

Easterners, on the other hand, have been more aware of movement as spiritual. The word yoga is actually derived from the Sanskrit root word "yuj" which means to yoke -- to join or unite. As oxen are yoked together, yoga joins the body and soul.

Yoga movements and breathing techniques were designed in ancient times to help one gain control of the "kundalini" or life force energy. By experiencing and controlling this spiritual life force energy, expanded awareness and realization of the True Self would manifest.

Today there are so many varieties of yoga. Some are physically oriented while others intend to evoke a mind/body/spirit experience. Some of the latter types engage in practices that are related to the Hindu while others have no religious affiliation.

I have included links in the Resource section to some online yoga sites. If you are interested, you might find it helpful to check out places that offer yoga classes. There you can ask questions that help you choose the type of yoga that fits you.

Alternatively, you might find some audio or video recordings of yoga classes that work for you.

Just as with guided meditation, once you become familiar with the breathing, movements, and poses, you will be able to do yoga as a spiritual practice on your own.

Walking the labyrinth

A labyrinth serves as a maze that takes us on a path for mind, body, and spirit transformation. More information and labyrinth locations can be found online at https://labyrinthsociety.org.

Labyrinth meditation played an important role in medieval spiritual life at the famous Chartres Cathedral in France. Grace Cathedral in San Francisco has a replica of their labyrinth.

Walking the labyrinth is a slow and intentional walk; it is a path winding inward and outward. The path has no dead-ends.

Labyrinth walking offers a deep form of meditation.

Practice: Labyrinth Walking

- ♥ Purgation/Releasing: Let go of the details of life. Release distractions. Let your thoughts drift off like clouds. Open your heart and quiet your mind; be aware of your breath with each step.

- ♥ Illumination/Receiving: When you have reached the center of the labyrinth, stay there as long as you wish. Meditate and pray. Receive what comes to you. You may also want to leave a symbol of gratitude at the center. Often times my friend leaves a rock from one of her mountain hikes. Remember to respect what others have left before you.

- ♥ Union/Returning: Leave the center and journey back to the "world" the same way that you came. Let the higher forces available to you through your true Self, The Divine, accompany you on your return. At this stage, strengthening your well-being and connecting to your Divine will take place if you so choose.

You can make your own labyrinth. A garden or backyard can be transformed into a labyrinth with stones. A large piece of canvas can be painted with a labyrinth -- roll it up and take it with you!

There are links in the Resource section to more information on labyrinths including places to order templates, portable labyrinths, blank labyrinth canvases, landscapers who create labyrinths, and locations of labyrinths throughout the world.

Postures

Posture as spiritual practice happens when you position your body in a way that calms your mind, body, and spirit to receive The Divine Presence within you.

You are already familiar with postures such as:

- ♥ Hands folded in prayer
- ♥ Kneeling
- ♥ Bowing the head

Postures, when practiced repeatedly, facilitate entry into a state of Divine connection.

Yoga Asanas

Yoga positions are called asanas. Originally the asana was a simple seated position. Over time, yogis developed more postures.

Yoga moves provide physical advantages such as releasing muscle tension, removing energy blocks, and increasing health through circulatory stimulation.

Asanas can also help with spiritual practice of meditation. People find asanas control vital energy and balance the mind so that meditation can be practiced in a deeper way. Besides assuming a posture for a length of time, asanas can be done in a series of flowing movements from one posture to another. Vinyasa yoga uses flowing yoga movements.

If you are interested in asanas, you can find a wealth of information in books, online, and classes offered by yoga teachers. Because yoga poses are considered to be so valuable, you'll find an abundant amount of information on yoga.

Hand postures

Mudras are ancient hand postures that have specific associations like inner peace or blessing. Perhaps you have seen paintings or sculptures with hands held in a mudra position.

The two most common mudras depicted in association with Jesus Christ include the hands held up and cupped forward symbolizing blessing. The other mudra has the tip of the thumb touching the index finger which represents the Gyan Mudra or Chin Mudra. The Chin Mudra signifies the unity of human consciousness with The Divine.

Practice: Gyan Mudra of Conscious Unity with The Divine

♥ Sit on a chair or cushion. Rest your hands on your knees with palms facing upward. Touch the tip of your index finger to the tip of your thumb. Your finger signifies you, the individual, while your thumb signifies The Divine Originating Source. Breathe in and out deeply as you sit quietly for one minute and longer if you wish.

Practice: Mudra Position to Calm the Mind for connecting to The Divine

♥ Sit cross-legged if you can do so comfortably; otherwise sit in a chair. Bend your arms in front of you, elbows up at chest level with your right hand resting on your left forearm and the back of your left hand touching the underside of your right forearm. Both palms will be facing the floor. Keep your fingers together and straight.

♥ While taking long, deep and slow breaths, hold this position for three minutes. Continue in peaceful stillness for longer if you wish.

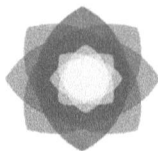

PART 3: LIVING

As your wisdom grows,
you will replace much of your fear with faith:
faith that all is well,
faith that life is in Divine order,
faith that there is Divine purpose to all that transpires, and
faith that in every challenge there is learning -- and
blessing.

--Marya L. OMalley
Minister, Teacher, Writer, Chiropractor, Life Coach

Chapter Ten: Encountering life

So often we come up against disruptions, distractions, and barriers. These "things" can drain our energy. Why? Because we are human. This chapter is intended to help you recognize these barriers so that you can begin to release them, reclaim your essential energy, and be more aware of your Divine nature.

The monkey mind means no harm

Often the "monkey mind" is just trying to prevent us from disengaging from ego control. The ego naturally tries to keep us anchored to fearful thinking by giving us the impression that this fearful place is safer. Ego serves as a protective mechanism that operates from a base of fear.

Just as the physical shadow is created by our bodies blocking the light, metaphorically many of us have been afraid of our own three dimensional physical existences. I wonder if this is the origin of *"being afraid of one's own shadow"*?

Neither can we rid ourselves of the ego, nor would it be beneficial to do so. The ego is a creation of the soul. It has a purpose – the ego anchors the soul in the physical body and makes navigation through life in the physical world possible. Ego emerges as the soul's incarnate physical life unfolds.

Ego protects our physical survival.

As wisdom grows, however, we will replace fear with faith: faith that all is well, that life is in Divine order, that there is Divine purpose to all that transpires and that in every challenge there is a lesson.

So, release the fear. Have courage, which really means *have heart*. The root word for courage is "cour" which means heart. The true loving Divine Self is not fearful; there is no fear in love.

Our hearts wait for us to unveil the next layer of love; to deepen the love we have for ourselves; to have faith.

Fear Itself

I grew up with the quote from President Franklin D. Roosevelt about having nothing to fear except "fear itself." I now understand.

Much suffering results from the illusion that we can control things that cannot be controlled. Many people wish to stop the constant change we experience in this world we live in. They hide in fear about life changes.

Spiritual practice helps us release our fears by willingly opening ourselves up to life. Everyone has some kind of struggle internally and externally. Let go of self-judgment and doubt. Free yourself.

Embracing your life means forgiving yourself. Forgive yourself and you will be able to forgive anyone, anywhere, anytime, past, present, and future. There is more to come later in this chapter about forgiveness.

Caution

Remember opening up to life requires you to continue with self-care and healthy boundaries. To be "spiritual" means to live with Divine Love. Be careful of people who want to steal your energy, waste your time, involve you in their melodramas, and abuse you or your loved ones.

Being a human doormat is not a life purpose or calling.

Feelings

Know that feelings just need to be felt and acknowledged. To feel doesn't mean you or I will act on our feelings.

Once feelings have been acknowledged, we are released and can move on. Feel your feelings as they arise. Remember emotions and feelings help us experience life fully.

If you are someone who doesn't know what you feel anymore due to habitually denying your feelings or suppressing them, engage in practices that help you to remember how to feel again.

If necessary, get professional help. The book by Karol Kuhn Truman, *Feelings Buried Alive Never Die*, is a good book on the subject. The Self -Awareness Meditation practice in Chapter 5 can help you reconnect with your feelings.

Substances and habits

Distractors surround us -- tobacco, food, alcohol, drugs, gambling, shopping and more. As distractors they keep us away from our feelings and being present in the moment.

Addiction to alcohol, drugs, sex, and compulsive activities like gambling or hoarding are disorders and considered to be diseases.

With alcohol addiction, the addict usually starts innocently drinking for fun with family and friends. Most people can handle the effects of alcohol – many cannot. Many people are genetically inclined to addiction. The effect of alcohol on the brain is so powerfully pleasant for them that they experience an instant attachment to the effect and continue to drink. Eventually they begin to self-medicate to obliterate their feelings.

So often people think that addiction is a moral issue, but is it? The three stages of addiction are:

1. Fun
2. Fun and problems, and finally
3. Problems

Many in recovery from alcoholism and addictions have done so by developing a spiritual connection with a higher power. For example, the 11th Step of Alcoholics Anonymous 12-step program involves improving "conscious contact" with God through prayer and meditation.

Electronics and digital media

Electronics and digital media can get in the way of spiritual development. We can keep our cell phones, laptops, gaming, Facebook, Twitter, and other social media – we just need to get rid of our over-attachment to them.

Like Russian physiologist Ivan Pavlov's dogs, we often react to these electronic stimuli by responding immediately – without thinking. That little sound or vibration from your mobile phone is so powerful that over time, we train our brains to stop everything and react immediately to the notifying noise.

Do you really need that photo of your friend's lunch? Will missing the call to schedule your appointment mean you will miss out? Relax. All these things can be addressed in time. Unleash yourself.

Whether you schedule a break from media or regularly just take a break, you need a break. Trust that it will all work out. Each of us has an internal compass to manage our lives. If you let your electronics and digital presence control your life, you lose.

Because of the complexity and speed of things today, we often make too many demands upon ourselves. When digital media demands take up so much time that we have little time left to meditate, enjoy family, pray, write, dance, walk, exercise, or do other uplifting activities, then it's time to cut back on the digital media time.

The world will not fall apart when a phone call goes unanswered.

If you are -- or suspect you are -- addicted to electronic devices like your smartphone, you can ask The Divine to help you release your addiction. Embrace your own dream of enlightenment and freedom. Release your attachments to answering that email, phone call, or text immediately.

Your friends and family will adjust and so will you. Let them know your – *fill in the blank* – will no longer control your day.

A Personal Story

As I wrote this book, I found myself being distracted with exploring great websites, writing to friends, posting updates, and more. Although I enjoyed what I was doing and received great satisfaction from communicating with loved ones, expanding my knowledge, and gaining insights to spiritual living – I realized that I maintained this activity for two or more hours a day if you count weekends.

I wanted to write this book!

I asked Divine Love and Wisdom for help to change my day's schedule to allow for more intentional living and less knee jerk reaction to bells, alarms, rings, vibrations, and buzzes.

I found that this happened automatically. As I aspired to eliminate time wasters, I returned to writing this book. If you desire to have more time for your true passions, set your intention and watch your higher Self work its magic.

Unnecessary busyness

Are you making multiple trips to take care of errands that could be lumped into one trip that would save time, gas, and money? I call this "unnecessary busyness."

Planning can save us from the distraction of last minute frenzy. For those of us who are easily distracted, we can learn to plan to keep us on track and have more time for ourselves and a better sense of well-being. I now make lists to follow.

Down Time

We all need "down time" to relax and rejuvenate ourselves. Let's be sure that the time we allow ourselves is restful or serves as an escape for play. Leisure time is best when it renews and refreshes. Focus on your heart's desires. Unplug.

> *You are what you love and*
> *you love what you give your attention to.*
>
> **--Vaishali**
> Spiritual Teacher and Life Management Expert

Financial headaches

In our culture, financial problems can be the greatest cause of anxiety. Financial problems are cited as the number one cause of divorce in the United States. If you over-extend yourself, stop to take care of yourself and honestly assess your finances.

Determine a budget -- expenses can be reduced and in some cases eliminated. There are helpful books on financial peace. See the reading list in the Reference section.

Remember to ask for financial guidance from The Divine.

Drama

You know what I mean. Maybe it is your drama or maybe you have friends or family members in your life who are the drama queens and kings. Drama takes time away from your soul's evolution.

If you find yourself as the center of the drama, seek guidance from your Divine Self. Practice meditation to listen to what's causing the drama in your life. If you need professional help and guidance, get it. You need to get your life back on track.

If you find yourself engaging in other people's drama, take healthy action to remove yourself from the situation. Know that some people thrive in their drama and constantly replace one for another. The one thing that you cannot buy is more time for yourself to enjoy life.

A good way to handle drama people is to express your confidence that they will be able to work it out, handle it well, and come through it all. Remind them to call upon their own Divine Source to help reset their internal compass. Soon they may find life clearing up for them, so that they can focus on their own happiness

It is not your responsibility to fix them; only they can fix themselves. Acknowledge that Divine Source is their Source as well as yours.

Time will be freed up for your own simply Divine life because your energy will be intact and available for you to use at will.

Martyrdom

It is not that we set out to be diverted from our dreams; it is that sometimes we allow ourselves to be diverted.

Martyrdom sacrifices personal Spiritual well-being out of a false sense of obligation, guilt, and need to control others by expecting something as a result of doing something "for" someone else. Martyrdom is misplaced attention and less than positive intention. The martyr is in effect making his or her happiness a condition of doing for others and is focused on others' reactions to the doing.

You've heard this line at the movies, "After all I did for you, and this is how you repay me?" That's how the martyr thinks. They think if they do this; you should do that.

Often the recipient of the martyr's service didn't even ask for it or want it. The martyr's service usually feels like meddling to the recipient.

Service in the spiritual sense does not mean sacrificing your personal health and well-being.

Sometimes there is a need to give of time and energy to and for others. When done consciously and in a spirit of conscious service rather than martyrdom, it is healthy and contributes to well-being.

The following chart shows some simple distinctions between compassionate service to others and unhealthy service.

Compassionate Service	Unhealthy Service
Share your food so that others might be nourished	Insist that others share their food
Service out of genuine caring	Service to manipulate others
Service without concern about what people think	Service to demonstrate superiority
Recognition isn't important	Service to get noticed

If you are martyring yourself, set your intention to stop wasting your time and energy in this manner. Ask for help from your true Source, The Divine. Ask to relate to others in a healthy way without expecting something in return for your doing, and without attempting to control others.

Realize that "martyrdom" is a distraction from your happiness, well-being, and soul evolution. Be compassionate to yourself. Look to better relationships and boundaries with others.

Find out about Al-Anon or other support groups if you are being a martyr around the addictions of others. Get professional help if you need it.

Willing or unwilling recipient of a martyr's services

If you receive the services of a martyr or martyrs in your life, pray for guidance and let the martyr know that you do care about him or her. Affirm you are the one that takes responsibility for you. You are responsible for your behavior, habits, health, how you raise children, handle finances, or cook food.

The martyr observes lack of responsibility -- real or not -- and tries to rescue others from consequences as if her/his survival depended upon it.

To be released, be honest with yourself and the martyr. Make it clear that you are responsible for yourself and the results of your actions. Kindly refuse the assistance.

If taking advantage of a martyr again and again, there is no right to complain about it. Be a self-responsible person. Use spiritual practice to connect with Divine Love and Wisdom. The guidance of Divine Love and Wisdom can only lead to healthy behaviors and better relationships.

False Guilt

Another distractor is a sense of false guilt related to taking on responsibility that is not ours. We can't take it on anyway, because the responsibility doesn't belong to us.

One of the main reasons people take on obligations of others is to make others happy. No one can make us happy; why do we think we can make others feel happy?

Claim what is yours and leave the rest! A conscious practice of this enables us to differentiate more and more where we assume false responsibility.

Healthy boundaries

We do not need to live in isolation from others. On the contrary, having healthy boundaries enables us to be truly intimate with others who also have healthy boundaries. Relationships with healthy boundaries will be clear and clean, free from manipulation. Self-responsible friends are required. Yes, those people are out there and you will find them when you are dedicated to being responsible for your own happiness.

This doesn't mean that you must cut off association with those who are still mired in inappropriately blaming other people for their circumstances/happiness. Rather, you will be able to make a conscious decision as to whether or not you want to continue a relationship with that person. If you do choose to continue a relationship, you will be able to identify and set healthy parameters of that relationship for yourself.

Healthy boundaries actually give us more freedom. With them there is more time for inspiration and activity such as writing a book, learning a language, taking vacations, meditating regularly, exercising, sleeping better, and enjoying the good company of friends and family.

A better question

If feeling blocked, take a look around. Are you making excuses and generating negative reasons? If so, you might benefit from asking yourself better questions.

The Universe is impartial to the questions we ask. It will answer any and all of our questions. The answers to better questions result in fresh and inspiring perspectives.

Stop asking, "Why am I – *fill in the negative status* --?"

Start asking questions like "How am I growing in Spirit? How am I successful? Why am I a blessing to others?" or any other questions that provide positive feedback. It's easier to be happy if you know what you are doing right and keep doing it.

By asking better questions, you will receive better answers. It is up to us to ask useful questions that will generate helpful answers.

Withholding forgiveness

For our health and well-being, we must forgive:

- ♥ Other people
- ♥ God
- ♥ Ourselves

Forgiving other people

Forgiveness frees us from paying the price that comes when we relive an injustice over and over again in our minds. Forgiving another will release us from the unjust or evil behavior we experienced with that person.

You hear it on the news where parents of a murdered child forgive the killer. They do not forgive because the killer deserves to be forgiven. The parents forgive because they deserve to feel compassion, self-love, and self-acceptance again.

Forgiving others is about forgiving yourself to live again.

Forgiving God

In *The Four Agreements*, Don Miguel Ruiz tells us that once we forgive God, we will be able to forgive ourselves as well. This, he says, is the end of self-rejection and the beginning of self-acceptance.

Maybe you are angry at God because you have experienced the tremendous pain of losing a loved one. Maybe you are angry at the Divine because you were treated unjustly.

There are many reasons that a person might harbor a personal grudge against The Divine as though The Divine is a person who has "done wrong" to them.

Life has loss, challenge, and heartache. It also has success, love, and happiness. Things happen because you live. You have control over how you react to what happens. Forgiveness is a choice.

Forgiving yourself

You have the ability to have compassion for yourself and to be accepting of yourself.

Maybe you are very good at it or maybe you're not.

If not, you can cultivate that ability. Spiritual practice will help and self -forgiveness will free you from the inner destructive critic that lives like a worm in your thoughts.

Practice: Forgiveness

- ♥ Make a habit of practicing forgiveness daily. This will help "keep the slate clean," so to speak.

- ♥ Each night before bed, review your day.

    1. Did you say, do, or think anything that you wish you hadn't? Are holding something against yourself?

    2. Think about it and determine whether there is anything for which you need to make amends.

    3. Make amends to yourself and take any action that is needed or make a to-do list for the earliest opportunity to make amends.

- ♥ Now review again for any actions or words that someone else did or said that you perceive as unfair, unjust, hurtful, harmful, etc.

- ♥ Review the situation; what was your role in it? Do you see the situation differently now, or the same way? Do you need to take any action in order to resolve it?

- ♥ Address the person in your mind. If addressing the person in your mind is too difficult or unimaginable, then address that person's higher Self through your higher Self. Tell them that you are forgiving them.

- ♥ Ask The Divine to surround them with a bubble of Divine love and release that bubble to the care and keeping of the Divine. Imagine the bubble floating higher and higher until it's gone from sight.

- ♥ Give thanks that you are now free and clear.

If you have imagery that suits you more than suggested here, by all means use it. The important thing is to forgive and be freed from resentment and anger's hold.

Forgiveness is so essential to our well-being because life involves many situations that feel unjust, insulting, or even evil. Forgiveness empowers us.

You will know when you have forgiven. Your buttons that once were pushed are gone. You will feel lighter. You will feel happier, renewed, empowered, and free. Make it a daily practice. I do.

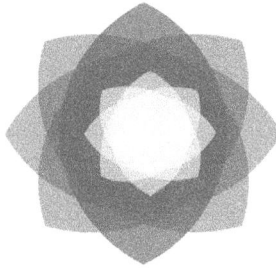

Choose to give your attention to The Divine within you.
Intend to know Divine Presence in your life.

--Marya L. OMalley
Minister, Teacher, Writer, Chiropractor, Life Coach

Contrary to what some think, change does not happen out of sheer will power. It blossoms out of intention. Intention is a force in the universe that allows creation to take place. Intention harnesses Source energy to make our dreams come true.

Divine Originating Source intends each of us to be here through the power of intention. In the same way that an oak tree comes from an acorn, you come from The Divine Source.

Dr. Wayne Dyer reminds us that the reality of the power of intention is that we don't attract what we want; we attract what we are. Remember the spiritual teacher Vaishali's quote "You are what you love and you love what you give your attention to." I believe this to be true.

Choose to give your attention to the Divine within you and intend to experience and know the Divine Source in your life. Choose to be enlightened.

Establish a Habit of Re-directing Your Attention when It Wanders

Be clear on your intentions. If you say what you want and then direct your attention to its opposite, what you really love is not what you say - - it's the opposite. Be clear about what you want.

As you progress along the way, you will find that you are in a conscious state of contact with the Divine more and more until this becomes a regular aspect of your daily living.

Do not expect to constantly be in a state of bliss, although it could happen. For most of us, human life is an ebb and flow.

Your regular practice will take you where you want to go if you have intent. Remember life is a field -- a field of opportunity for creating awareness, happiness, and a good life.

Divine living is a lifestyle.

Only you know what right looks like for you. Your being is a unique being of Divine consciousness.

Be responsible and hold your intention. Consciously keep your thoughts and actions aligned with your intentions.

Remember to take breaks. Rest and relaxation serve an important part of healthy integrated living.

A checklist for simply Divine living

1. Make a commitment.

2. Engage daily in regular practice.

3. Relax -- practice, allow, observe, and release.

4. Observe; don't judge.

5. Ask and you shall receive.

6. Troubleshoot as needed; work with challenges.

7. Forgive.

8. Honor yourself in all that you say and do.

9. Remember you are simply Divine!

There is no cut and dried formula for you as a Divine being. Divine Love and Wisdom will always be available to you. Know that other teachers have ways to show up when you need them.

> *Although you appear in earthly form,*
> *your essence is pure consciousness.*
> *You are the fearless guardian of Divine Light.*
> **-- Rumi**
> 13th Century Persian Poet and Islamic Scholar

May you enjoy your simply Divine life!

Thank you.

The Divine You unfolds.
Visit often to recharge.

REFERENCING

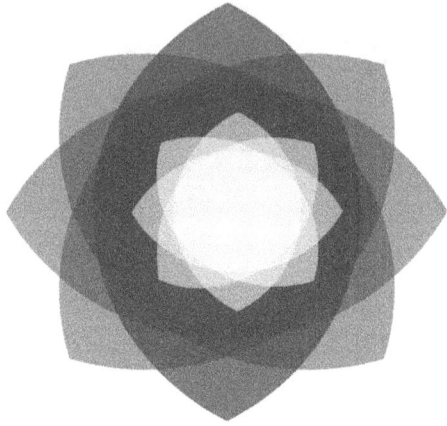

You are simply Divine

Other names for The Divine

Divine Presence
Divine Source
Divine Love and Wisdom
Divine Mind
God/Goddess
God Force
The Universe
Universal Source
Infinite Source
Spirit
Holy Spirit
Great Spirit
Spirit of the Universe
Supreme Being
Higher Power
Creator
The Absolute

Ever-Present Origin
Ultimate Reality
Causeless Cause
Great I Am
The Tao
Original Essence
All That Is
Yahweh
Atman
Brahma
Ahura Mazda
Adonai
The Field
Great Mystery
Infinite Intelligence
The One Originating Source

You may know of other names for The Divine;
feel free to jot them down here.

Words and their meanings

Accepting: To acknowledge without judging

Awareness: To realize that something, someone, or an experience exists | Synonym: **Consciousness**

Blessing: To wish the best for another person, place, or thing; to acknowledge and honor an individual's worth

Body: To express awareness through the physical world

Consciousness: To gain a sense of awareness; to realize an idea, object, or condition; the sum total of all ideas and experiences accumulated by a person that affects her/his present being

Contemplating: To concentrate on the spirit as a private devotion; to transcend into a state of spiritual awareness

Distractors: People, places, things, and thoughts that pull you away from experiences of greater awareness

The Divine: That whichever was is and shall be -- The One Originating Source | Refer to *Names for The Divine* | Synonym: **God**

Divine Love and Wisdom: Another name for The One Originating Source used when emphasizing the qualities of love and wisdom

Divine Mind: Another name for The One Originating Source used when experiencing "one mind" with The Divine through spiritual living

Divine Presence: Another name for The One Originating Source used when emphasizing the omnipresence of The Divine in our consciousness

Divine Will: Pure spiritual energy of love manifesting in creation; it supports soul evolution and transcends ego domination

Ego: A creation of the soul that emerges as physical life unfolds; makes navigation through physical life possible

Energy: A universal force within every person, place or thing existing in all dimensions

Entity: A self-contained person, place, thing, or thought that exists

Essence: The underlying core of what truly is

Faith: To place trust in something or someone without proof; A living trust in the existence of The Divine

Free Will: The human faculty to choose outside of instinct and without Divine intervention

Frequency: The rate at which something vibrates and repeats itself

Gap: The space between thoughts that allows for conscious contact with The Divine Self

Heart Center: The place between the breasts and underneath the sternum which serves as your heart energy center while meditating or moving through yoga poses

Holy Spirit: Another name for The One Originating Source used when emphasizing the qualities of wisdom, knowledge, and understanding; Divine knowledge that can recognize all the ego has invented and inform us of Divine reality.

Instinct: Unlearned natural movement, thought, or action; a natural ability

Intend: To knowingly take action

Journaling: To record thoughts, stories, and experiences through the written word; often accompanied with mementos

Light: Emanation of Divine energy; In the *Book of Genesis*, God created light first

Meditate: Attention focused inward; to listen to the inner Divine

Mindfulness: To practice maintaining a heightened or even complete awareness of one's inner and outer worlds without casting judgment

Monkey Mind: Your monkey mind is negative chatter often encompassing your darkest fears; one's ego voice

Originating Source and **Universal Source:** Names for The One Originating Source used by those who prefer names free of traditional meanings

Prayer: To talk with and listen to The One Originating Source; the communion of the soul with The Divine

React: To take action or develop a thought in response to something or someone

Reflect: To concentrate on a subject that can lead to self-understanding or insight

Resonate: To be in harmony with life's vibration

Release: To let something go

Sacred: To value a person, place, thing, or thought with the highest of importance

Sacred Words: Words used in meditation and prayer; Love, Allah, Shalom, Yahweh, Peace, Wisdom, Spirit, and others

Self: with an upper case "S" represents the Impersonal Self or The Divine Eternal Self

self: with a lower case "s" represents the personal self -- the ego or "little self"

The Silence and **The Stillness:** The space between thoughts where the present moment resides; a state of inner quiet when the mind is at rest

The Soul: The sum total of your conscious and subconscious minds now and through all lifetimes.

Soul Evolution: The unfolding of The Divine Self in our consciousness

Spirit: Another name for The One Originating Source used when emphasizing our true nature in the visible and invisible eternal worlds

Spirituality: To understand one's true nature; one may be spiritual without religious affiliation

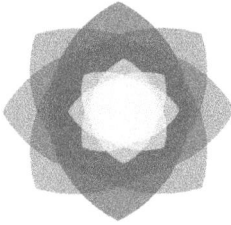

QUOTES

Chapter 1: Who are you?
Eckhart Tolle -- Spiritual Teacher and Author

Chapter 2: Why are you here?
Marya OMalley -- Handbook Author

Chapter 3: Your evolving soul
Wayne Dyer -- Author and Motivational Speaker
http://www.drwaynedyer.com/articles/you-are-god-an-in-depth-conversation-with-dr-wayne-dyer, retrieved 11/11/2013

Chapter 4: Your spiritual growth
Dr. Joe Dispenza -- Researcher, Lecturer, Chiropractor, and Author

Marya OMalley -- Handbook Author

Chapter 5: Meditating ways
Thich Nhat Nanh -- Zen Master
http://www.psychologytoday.com/blog/here-there-and-everywhere/201206/36-quotes-meditation, retrieved 9/12/14

Chapter 6: Initiating prayer
Mary-Alice and Richard Jafolla -- Spiritual Authors and Golf Enthusiasts
http://www.unity.org/resources/articles/prayer

Chapter 7: Blessing your life
Pierre Pradervand – Author and Spiritual Leader
The Gentle Art of Blessing

Chapter 8: Keeping your journal
Christina Baldwin – Author, Speaker, and Educator
http://www.goodreads.com/quotes/tag/journaling

Adam L. Feldman – Pastor, Church Planter Coach, and Writer
Journaling: Catalyzing Spiritual Growth Through Reflection

Chapter 9: Moving your soul
Martha Graham – Choreographer and Mother of Modern Dance
http://clevelandclinicwellness.com/mind

Chapter 10: Encountering life
Marya OMalley -- Handbook Author

Vaishali – Spiritual Teacher and Life Management Expert

Chapter 11 Living your Divine
Marya OMalley -- Handbook Author

Rumi – 13th Century Persian Poet and Islamic Scholar

Bible quotes in this book are from The Green Bible (2008), (NRSV, 1989), Harper One of Harper Collins Publishers, made gender neutral by the author

READINGS

Enjoy reading these books by various spiritual leaders and thinkers who have influenced my Divine.

- ♥ An Easy Guide to Meditation, Roy Eugene Davis

- ♥ Assertiveness for Earth Angels, Doreen Virtue

- ♥ Birthing a Greater Reality: A Guide for Conscious Evolution, Robert Brumet

- ♥ Blessing, The Art and Practice, David Spangler

- ♥ Dance, The Sacred Art: The Joy of Movement as Spiritual Practice, Cynthia Winton-Henry

- ♥ The Divine Name, (book and CD), Jonathan Goldman

- ♥ Even Mystics Have Bills to Pay, Jim Rosemergy

- ♥ The Gentle Art of Blessing, Pierre Pradervand

- ♥ Getting in the Gap: Making Conscious Contact with God through Meditation (book and CD), Wayne Dyer

- ♥ Handbook of Positive Prayer, Hypatia Hasbrouck

- ♥ Heart-Centered Metaphysics: A Deeper Look at Unity Teachings, Paul Hasselbeck

- ♥ Higher Self Voices: Neutralizing Your Negative Thoughts and Emotional Blueprints, Janet Richmond

- ♥ Intimacy with God, Fr. Thomas Keating

- ♥ Jewish Meditation, Rabbi Aryeh Kaplan

- Journaling: Catalyzing Spiritual Growth Through Reflection, Adam Feldman

- Lessons in Truth, Emily Cady

- Living the Mystical Life Today, Jim Rosemergy

- Meditation for Dummies, 2nd edition, Stephan Bodian

- Meditation: Your Key to Accessing Universal Consciousness, Jane E. Hart

- 8 Minute Meditation: Quiet Your Mind, Change Your Life, Victor Davich

- The Power of Intention, Wayne Dyer

- A Spirituality of Imperfection, Henry Nowuen

- The Spirituality of Imperfection: Storytelling and the Search for Meaning, Ernest Kurtz and Katherine Ketchum

- Spiritual Power Tools, Jane E. Hart

- Wisdom Rising, volumes I and II, Vaishali

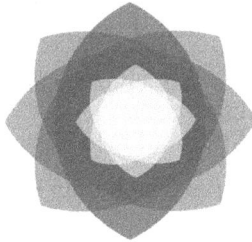

Resources

www.YOUAreSimplyDivine.com

Experiencing the silence within:

- ♥ http://www.unity.org/resources/articles/silence

Experiencing the gap between thoughts:

- ♥ http://www.abundancetapestry.com/experiencing-the-gap/

- ♥ The Places That Scare You: A Guide to Fearlessness in Difficult Times, Pema Chödrön, page 130 Loving-Kindness Practice

- ♥ Alan Cohen quoted by Psychology Today Magazine on the gap between thoughts at http://www.psychologytoday.com/blog/here-there-and-everywhere/201206/36-quotes-meditation

Body movement spiritual practice:

- ♥ http://episcopalcredo.org/CREDO2/assets/File/GUIDE_to_Spiritual_Practice_Body_Movement.pdf

- ♥ http://www.clevelandclinicwellness.com/mind/AMeaningfulLife/Pages/MovementAsSpiritualPractice.aspx

- ♥ Columbia Pictures, The Karate Kid

Yoga and Meditation:

- Meditation for Beginners with Maritza. Maritza (actor/ yoga instructor), Ted Landon (director), DVD. Note: This DVD has a 15-minute yoga track for relaxing and focusing, a 20-minute body scan, and a 20-minute seated meditation

- http://www.yogajournal.com/article/beginners/not-all- yoga-is-created-equal/

- http://life.gaiam.com/article/beginners-guide-8-major- styles-yoga

- Abraham Lincoln's meditation on Divine Will http:// www.abrahamlincolnonline.org/lincoln/speeches/ meditat.htm

- Rabbi Aryeh Kaplan, Jewish Meditation

- Free online music videos for meditation, sleep, and relaxation from Yellow Brick Cinema at http:// www.youtube.com/playlist? list=PLQkQfzsIUwRYn8ruamKgZi4sF1LNWb7Df

- Free online music for meditation at http://11radio.com/11 -meditation-and-health

Prayer:

- Affirmative prayer adapted from these websites: http:// keystoheaven.com/prayer/5-step.htm

- http://divineunity.org/keys/prayer.htm

Centering Prayer:

- Keating, Thomas. http://www.cpt.org/files/WS%20-% 20Centering%20Prayer.pdf

- Paul Hasselbeck, Heart Centered Metaphysics

Labyrinth walking meditation:

- http://www.wikihow.com/Meditate-in-a-Labyrinth
- http://www.labyrinthos.net/photo_library14.html
- http://www.labyrinthos.net/photo_library13.html See this link for labyrinth design images including those that vary from the round labyrinth at Chartres.
- http://www.labyrinthcompany.com/?gclid=CNDBmta_kcMCFaU7MgodZSsACQ This is a catalogue of labyrinth designs, stencils, templates and landscapers.
- http://labyrinthsociety.org/about-labyrinths
- http://labyrinthlocator.com/

Addiction:

- Alcoholics Anonymous (AA) on the 12 Steps: http://www.aa.org/pages/en_US/read-the-big-book-and-twelve-steps-and-twelve-traditions
- Improving conscious contact with God, the 11th step of AA meditation: http://11thstepmeditation.org/welcome.php
- http://na-recovery.org/
- http://www.rehabs.com/pro-talk-articles/if-not-aa-then-what-alternatives-to-12-step-groups/

Mudra practices:

- ♥ Yoga for the Hands: Sabrina's Mudra Cards. Sabrina Mesko. Andrews McMeel Publishing.

Forgiveness exercise:

- ♥ http://www.emoclear.com/forgivenessexercise.htm

Financial troubleshooting and debt-free living:

- ♥ The Complete Cheapskate: How to Get Out of Debt, Stay Out, and Break Free from Money Worries Forever, Mary Hunt.
- ♥ Debt Proof Living, Mary Hunt
- ♥ 7 Money Rules for Life, Mary Hunt
- ♥ Zero Debt, Lynette Kahlfani-Fox

Helpful apps for Android and iPhone:

- ♥ Attitudes of Gratitude Journal
- ♥ My Gratitude Journal
- ♥ Gratitude Journal and Community
- ♥ Insight Meditation Timer
- ♥ Bodhi Timer

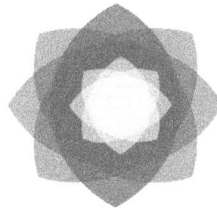

May The Divine within you awaken daily.

EXTRAS
MORE
AFFIRMING
MEDITATING
PRAYING

Affirming my Good

- ♥ Spiritual life is my priority and all the loving forces of the universe are supporting me.

- ♥ I call upon the Holy Spirit to inspire and inform my every thought, word, and action.

- ♥ I intend to see, feel, perceive, and interpret this differently for my highest good.

- ♥ Through intention I direct Source energy.

- ♥ My body is a Divine instrument.

- ♥ I am one with Divine Source.

- ♥ Fears and negative blueprints are neutralized now by Divine Source Light.

- ♥ This situation is working for me!

- ♥ I am simply Divine

MEDITATING CENTER

- Find a comfortable place to sit or stand in your home, garden, office, or any space that gives you privacy.

- Now close your eyes and breathe in, inhaling into your heart center. As you exhale, release anything ambient noise that bothers and any internal sensation that is causing you to hold tension in your body. Notice and release.

- Now when you next inhale, gather yourself upright. Lift your chin up so that it is parallel to the floor. Close your eyes and exhale while remaining up-right.

- Notice, as you continue to breathe, your physical center and then your Spirit center. They may be one in the same; they may be in different locations.

- Continue to breathe and notice them coming closer together if they were apart. When together, notice the location growing stronger, brighter, and more vibrant. You might feel yourself vibrating there.

- Continue to breathe, notice and experience.

- The center may have a sensation, color, warmth, or radiance that spreads. Let it do so. Feel that you have no bounds; the extent of your being is limitless in Divine Presence.

- Allow your light to extend outward, expanding to include the room, the building, the area outside, the state, the country, the world, the planet, further expanding outward into the Universe.

- Continue to breathe, notice and experience. Then bring your attention back to your body, the room, or wherever you are located. Relax and if time, journal about your experience.

PRAYING

Divine One Prayer

Divine One,

Ever present everywhere and within,

Hallowed omnipresence,

I dwell in the universe of Love,

Universe without division,

Between heaven and earth,

Between brother and sister,

Between stranger and stranger,

May I live awake in my right Divine Mind,

Free of the illusions of ignorance,

In expression of Divine Love and Wisdom.

Amen.

Inviting The Divine One

- ♥ Divine One, I invite you to help with the writing of this book inspired by the Holy Spirit and guided by Divine Will.

- ♥ I invite you, Holy Spirit, to inspire my every thought word and deed.

- ♥ Ultimate Source, creator of all, within right timing, create an opening in me to give and receive love in sacred intimate relationship with another person.

- ♥ Divine Presence, I open myself to Divine organization and inspiration to complete my plans and projects for the highest good of all.

- ♥ Lead me to people and places that will assist me in my work, Divine Source.

- ♥ Show me my next step and deliver me from the confusion I am experiencing, Divine One. I invite you to direct and guide me now.

- ♥ Divine One, I lift myself up in prayer to release any resentments that I am holding from the past and assist me in forgiving all those who have hurt me including, and foremost, myself.

- ♥ As I enter into this endeavor, Divine One, I invite you to guide me to make peace with my past and make amends with all.

The end is the beginning.

ABOUT THE AUTHOR

Marya L. OMalley serves as minister, teacher, writer, chiropractor, intuitive, and life coach. She brings her years of experience in human and spiritual development to life in this easy to use handbook on Divine Living. She provides useful stories to help you get grounded on the why behind living a Divine Life. She shares knowledge of others with relevant quotes. She also offers easy to follow practices to get you started and help you improve your Divine Life.

Her personal mission is to inspire her readers and clients to higher levels of consciousness and happiness through combining spiritual practice and everyday life. She does this with a holistic approach to serving others.

Dr. O'Malley was awarded a Master of Art Degree in Human Development and a Spirituality and Holistic Health certificate by St. Mary's University of Minnesota in 2002. She completed a unit of chaplaincy at United Hospital in St. Paul, Minnesota also in 2002 where she was part of the care team in the Intensive Care Unit, Oncology, and Surgery areas. She has an associate's degree in Minister of Spiritual Counseling through the New Seminary, New York, NY, which is accredited by the State University of New York (SUNY). She is also a certified hypnotherapist since 2001 with an emphasis on holistic health applications.

Marya has authored over 20 online and live courses for health care professionals. Through the years, she has united in marriage over 500 couples. As an intuitive she uses her gifts to provide insight to her clients regarding spiritual life, relationships, departed loved ones, decisions, and finances.

Meditating, praying, forgiving, and Divine Living have become a part of her daily personal spiritual practice. Connect with Marya on Facebook at Youaresimplydivine.

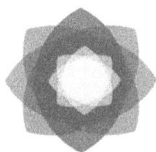

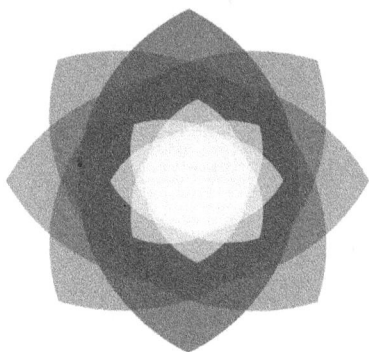

www.YouAreSimplyDivine.com

www.ingramcontent.com/pod-product-compliance
Lightning Source LLC
Chambersburg PA
CBHW052123090426
42741CB00009B/1927